SCHIRMER'S LIBRARY
OF MUSICAL CLASSICS

Vol. 2099

FRANZ WOHLFAHRT

Fifty Easy Melodious Studies
For the Violin, Op. 74

Books I and II

ISBN 978-1-4768-7568-2

G. SCHIRMER, Inc.

DISTRIBUTED BY

HAL•LEONARD®
CORPORATION
7777 W. BLUEMOUND RD. P.O. BOX 13819 MILWAUKEE, WI 53213

www.schirmer.com
www.halleonard.com

CONTENTS

Fifty Easy Melodious Studies, Op. 74

Fifty Easy Melodious Studies
Op. 74, Book I

Franz Wohlfahrt
(1833–1884)

Allegro moderato

2.

Allegro moderato

3.

Allegro moderato

4.

10

Moderato assai

13.

14

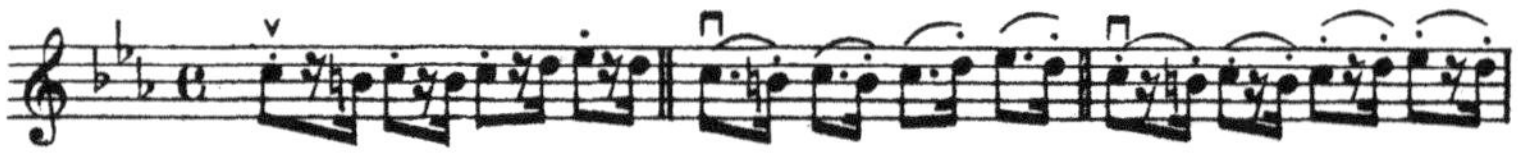

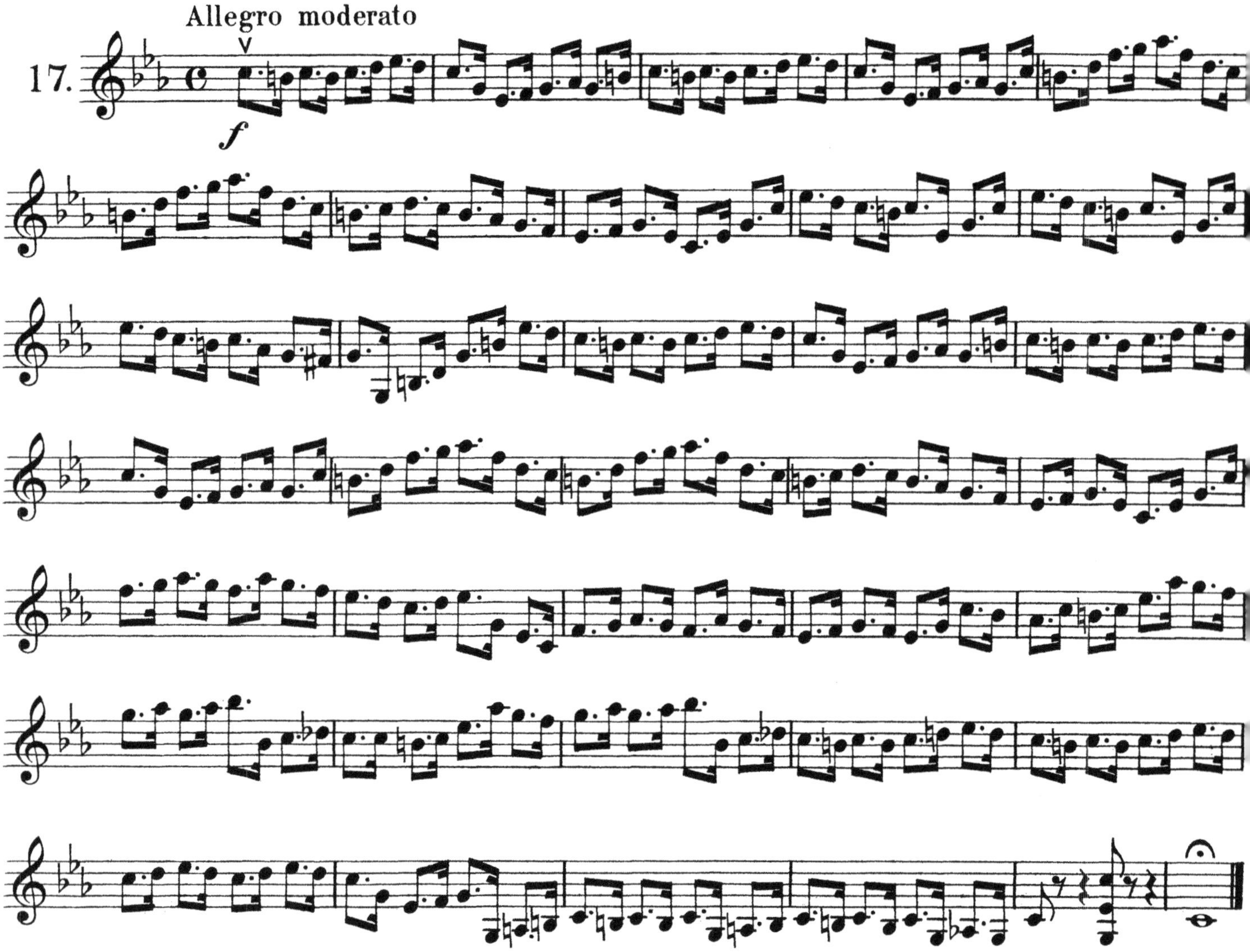
Allegro moderato
17.
f

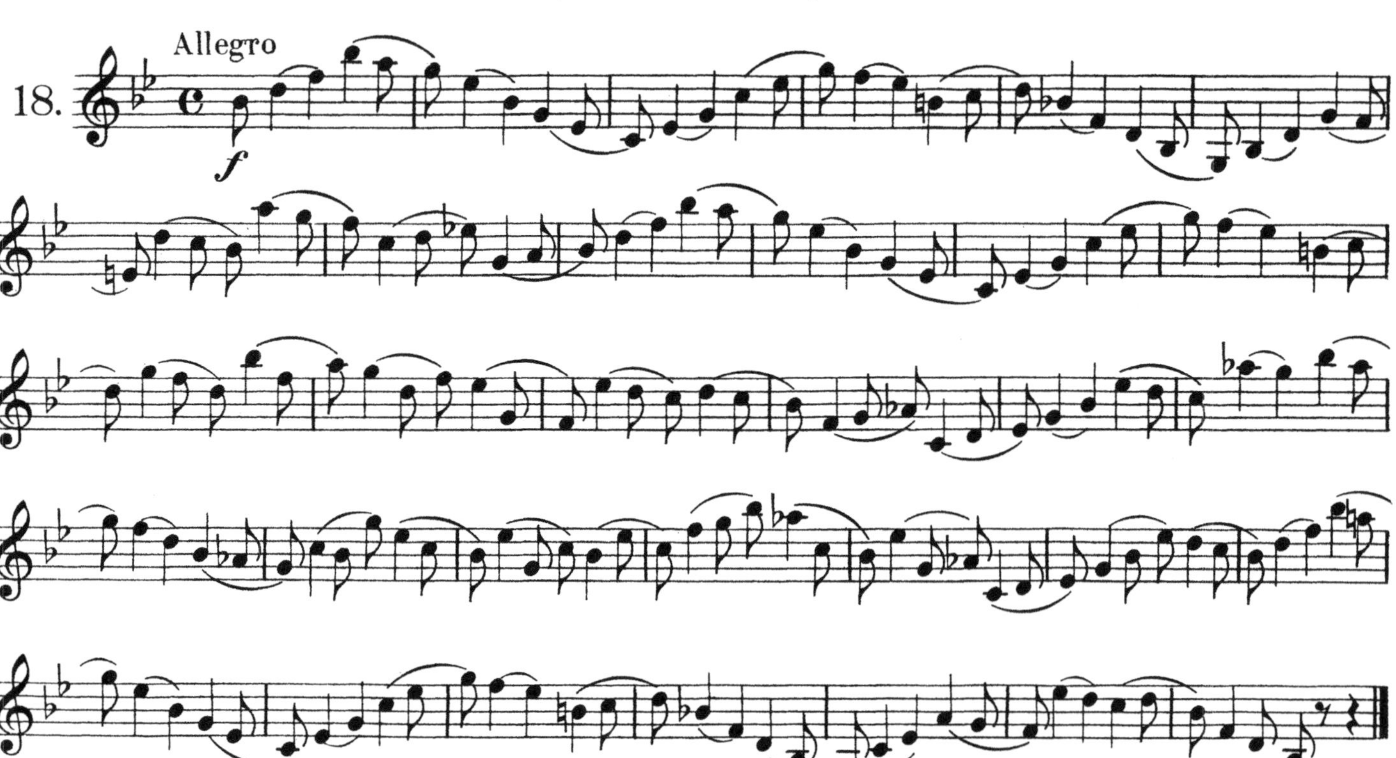
Allegro
18.
f

Fifty Easy Melodious Studies
Op. 74, Book II

Franz Wohlfahrt
(1833–1884)

32. Allegro moderato

28

35. Allegretto

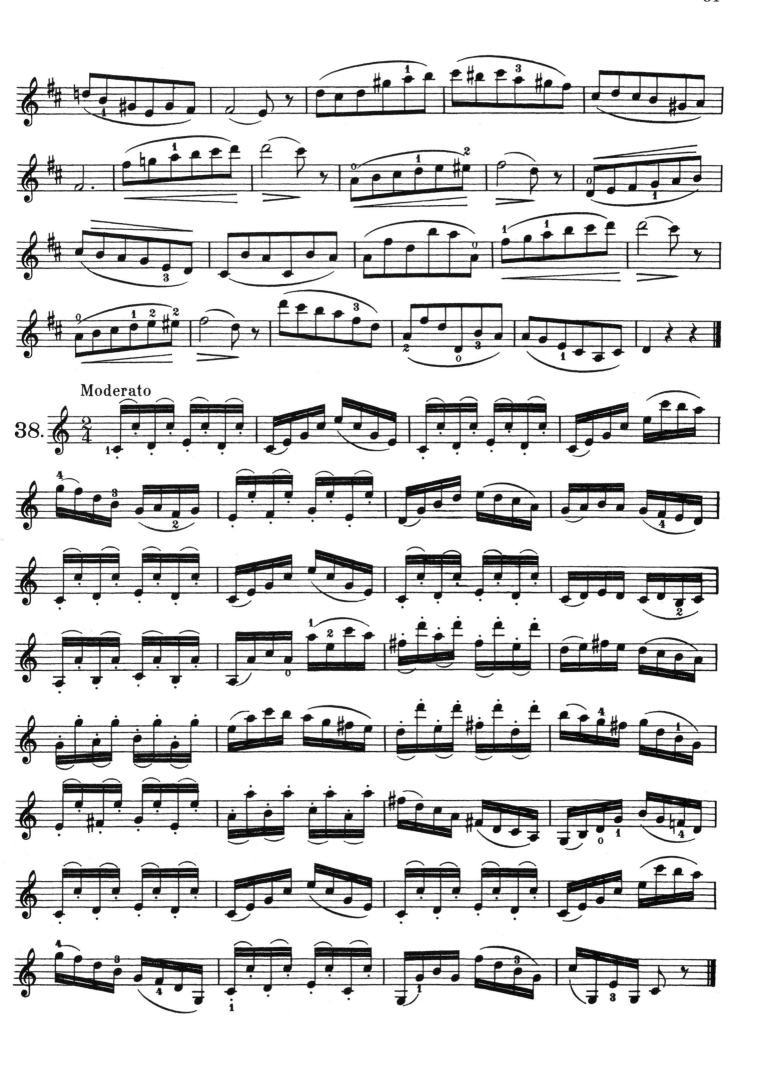

Moderato

38.